#2

TRIGUN YASUHIRO NIGHTOW

DEEP SPACE PLANET FUTURE GUN ACTION!!

内藤泰弘
YASUHIRO NIGHTOW

TRANSLATION
JUSTIN BURNS
LETTERING
STUDIO CUTIE

BARNES & NOBLE BOOKS
NEW YORK

PUBLISHERS
MIKE RICHARDSON
AND HIKARU SASAHARA

EDITORS
TIM ERVIN-GORE
AND FRED LUI

COLLECTION DESIGNER
DAVID NESTELLE

English-language version produced
by **DARK HORSE COMICS** and
DIGITAL MANGA PUBLISHING.

TRIGUN vol. 2

**This edition published exclusively for Barnes & Noble, Inc.
by Dark Horse Manga, a division of Dark Horse Comics, Inc.
and Digital Manga Publishing.**

**First edition: December 2004
ISBN: 0-7607-6866-8**

**10 9 8 7 6 5 4 3 2 1
Printed in China**

トライガン#2
DEEP SPACE PLANET FUTURE GUN ACTION!!

TRIGUN

内藤泰弘
YASUHIRO NIGHTOW

#2 TRIGUN YASUHIRO NIGHTOW
DEEP SPACE PLANET FUTURE GUN ACTION!!
CONTENTS

SUCH
A
BEAUTIFUL
DAY...

...

...

OH CRAP!

ARE YOU OKAY?

WHATCHA DOIN'?

SORRY! SORRY!

SHEESH...

SWEET!!

REALLY?!

C'MON, LET'S GET SOME ICE CREAM!

SIX, OK?

EH?!

ME TOO!

ME...

WHY NOT? YOU'RE *IMMATURE* ENOUGH...

HOW COME? ISN'T THAT ONE TOO MANY?

WANT TO COME PLAY WITH US?

WHA--?

JUST NOW, VASH LOOKED SO SERIOUSLY SAD...

WHAT WAS THAT...

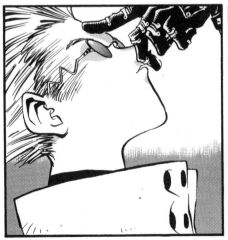

CHK

WHERE IS HE?

I'M THE ONE ASKING THE QUESTIONS.

WHERE IS HE?!

WHAT WOULD YOU DO IF I TOLD YOU?

....

....

25

I STILL HAVEN'T GIVEN YOU...

...YOUR GIFT, HAVE I?

MWA HA HA...

A **STRONGER** REACTION THAN I EXPECTED. HOW AMUSING!!

I COULD KILL **EVERY SINGLE** PERSON WITHIN FIFTY METERS OF HERE IN UNDER TWO SECONDS.

SHOULD I DESIRE...

YOU...

Y--

29

I'LL SET IT RIGHT HERE.

A LESSON FROM ME TO YOU.

THE REST IS A PARTING GIFT.

KYAAAAAAAAAAAAAAA!

DID YOU THINK IT WAS THE *DRUNKEN RAMBLING* OF AN *OLD MAN?*

HEH!

I ALMOST DID, YEAH.

SO, YOU REALLY *DID* SHOW UP.

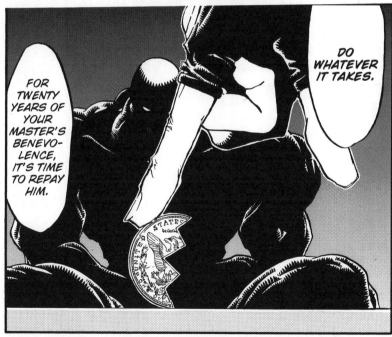

#1. BLOOD AND THUNDER/END

36

#2. DIABLO

I'VE FINALLY PICKED UP YOUR SCENT...

DON'T WRITE ME OFF.

I'LL TRACK YOU DOWN. I WON'T LET YOU GET AWAY.

KNIVES...

COUNT ON IT!!

40

HERE
AGAIN,
HUH?

VASH.

REM...

THIS SHIP IS *TOO* QUIET.

WHY IS EVERYONE STILL SLEEPING?

VASH...

...YOU AND ME, REM.

IT'S JUST YOU...

PROJECT *"SEEDS"*

THERE'S SOMETHING WRITTEN ON THE OUTSIDE OF THIS SHIP.

?

THESE SHIPS ARE *SEEDS* THAT THE HUMAN RACE BUILT TO CARRY OUR GENES TO AN UNKNOWN WORLD.

YOU COULD SAY THAT WE'RE THE *CARETAKERS* OF THESE SEEDS.

...BUT IT'S JUST OUR WILL TO *SURVIVE.*

IT MAY SEEM SILLY OR SHAMEFUL...

IF THERE'S A GOD IN DEEP SPACE, HE MIGHT *CHUCKLE* AT OUR SAD LITTLE STRUGGLE FOR *IMMORTALITY.*

44

YOU AND *KNIVES* ARE HERE.

I'M FINE.

DOESN'T THAT MAKE YOU SAD?

REM...

SHE SAID IF SHE WAS ALONE, ANY PLACE WAS THE SAME.

SO SHE LEFT ON THIS SHIP.

SHE LOVED THE EARTH, BUT THE ONES SHE CARED FOR HAD DIED.

REM WENT ON AHEAD OF THEM.

HOT TEARS STUNG MY EYES.

WHEN REM DIED, I HAD PLENTY OF TIME TO THINK ON IT.

HOW DOES IT FEEL WHEN SOMEONE YOU *LOVE* DIES?

I'M RIGHT NEXT TO YOU.

I WON'T LEAVE YOU ALL ALONE!

REM!

REM!

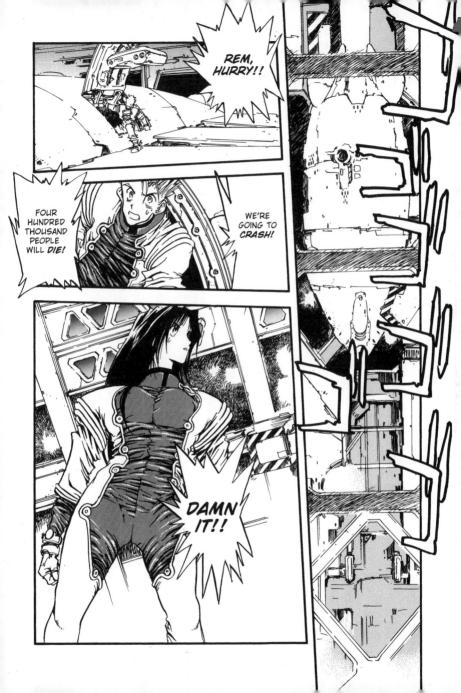

THAT WAS THE LAST TIME I SAW REM.

THE MOTHER SHIP SPARKLED AND SPLINTERED, SPINNING AS IT FELL OFF INTO THE DARKNESS.

KNIVES, YOU...

WHAT'S SO *FUNNY?*

HA HA HA HA!

HA!!

HA!!

HA!

HEH!

HEH HA!

I'M GLAD SHE'S GONE!

I THOUGHT I'D SPARE HER, BUT NOW I SEE SHE WAS *JUST AS FLAWED.*

THEY *WASTE* THEIR LIVES ON *FOOLISH FEELINGS!*

HUMANS ARE RIDICULOUS.

DIS-GUSTING!

THAT'D BE LIKE RELEASING A VIRUS INTO OUR BEAUTIFUL UNIVERSE!

LIKE I'D LET THEM EMIGRATE!

52

53

GRRK!

...
...

VASH-SAN?

OH...

IT'S YOU TWO.

THANK YOU.

BUT DON'T WASTE YOUR TIME.

THIS SHERIFF IS *SO* STUBBORN...

I'M TERRIBLY SORRY.

HEY, *WATCH IT!*

JUST SIT TIGHT AND WE'LL BE BACK FOR YOU TOMORROW.

YESSS?

U... UMM...

VASH-SAN?

BUT...!! YOU DIDN'T DO ANYTHING!!

... ...

NEVER MIND!!!

AH...

UM...

SOME-
THING'S
COMING!

WHAT
?!

EH?

!!

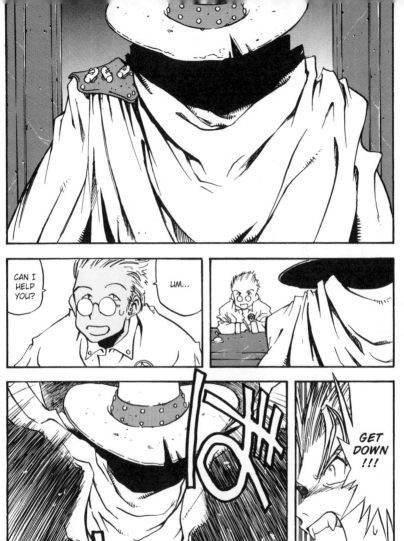

CAN I HELP YOU?

UM...

GET DOWN !!!

MY NAME IS *MONEV THE GALE!!*

I'M NUMBER ONE OF THE *GUNG-HO GUNS!!*

EVERY-ONE! HURRY UP AND *RUN!*

HE'S AIMING FOR ME!

VASH-SAN!!

BUT...

SHUT YOUR MOUTH!

STAY OUT OF IT! HURRY! OUTSIDE!

-≥KOFF!≤-

-≥KOFF!≤-

61

TWENTY YEARS IS A LONG TIME...

DAY IN AND DAY OUT OF *TRAINING HELL.*

SE--

SEMPAI!*

* SEMPAI = SENIOR, UPPERCLASSMAN.

...ONCE I KILL YOU!!

ALL THAT TRAINING'S GONNA PAY OFF...

69

#3

WITH EACH STEP, HE'S TWO DEGREES FURTHER...!!

HE'LL NEVER COME BACK ...!!

I CAN'T LET HIM GO...

VASH-SAN!!

VASH-SAN!!

NOW HIS FIREPOWER IS CUT IN HALF...

YOU DID IT!!

HIS *TASTE* FOR DESTRUCTION ISN'T GONE YET.

HE'S MORE POWERFUL THAN JUST THAT RIGHT ARM.

THIS IS BAD NEWS...

...SHERIFF.

WHERE
DID HE
GO...?

WHERE...

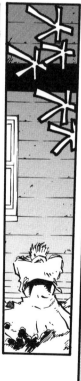

TAKE COVER!!

GWAA!

...!

WHY?!

→HEE!←

→HEE HEE!←

WHY IS HIS AIM SO PRECISE?

→GUH!←

WHAT A NIGHTMARE!!

THIS BASTARD'S CRAZY...

STAY AWAY!

IT'S DANGER-OUS, YOU IDIOT!!

VASH-SAN!!

PLANT SHIP'S ORBITAL TRAJECTORY CORRECTED.

WHAT?!

....
....

IT CAN'T BE!

COMING FROM THE FALLING MOTHER SHIP'S HOST COMPUTER...

FLEET'S AUTO-CRUISE SYSTEMS DISABLED. TRANSFERRING PLANT SHIPS TO PROGRAM CONTROL.

A FORCED OVER-RIDE?!

WHAT'S THAT?!

IMPOSSIBLE...

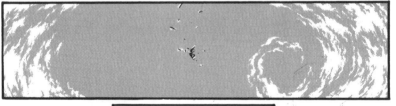

NOW!!

I NEED ACCESS TO YOUR SAFE.

OPEN. THAT. SAFE.

89

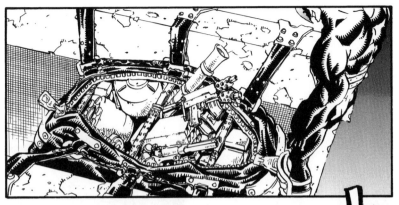

I'M GONNA *SMASH YOU* INTO TINY PIECES...

...VASH THE STAMP-EDE!!

91

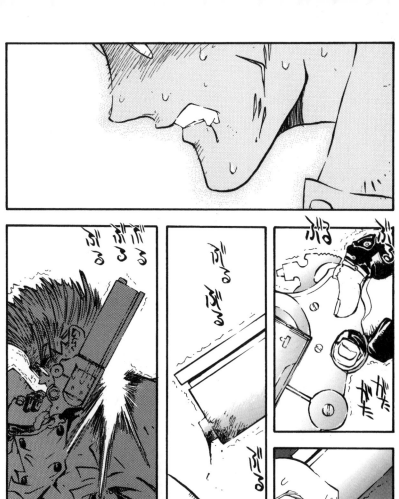

...THEN
SHE'LL
DIE.

IF I
SHOOT
HIM
NOW...

REM...

#3. FRAGILE ／ END

#4

THROUGH-OUT THE REBUILDING, TENSION SIMMERS IN THIS SMALL TOWN.

IT'S BEEN TWO DAYS SINCE ALL THAT *CHAOS.*

THE REASON HE'S CALLED THE *"HUMANOID TYPHOON"*...

IT'S MADE ME REALIZE SOME-THING...

BEING AROUND THE *REAL VASH THE STAMPEDE* MADE ME FORGET ABOUT HIS *REPUTA-TION*...

—HUHH—

...

AR--

AREN'T YOU GONNA *SHOOT ME?!*

—HAHH...—

THE MAN I THOUGHT WAS MY FATHER WAS JUST AN AGENT.

I WAS...

BOUGHT...

WHERE'S YOUR BOSS?

JUST HOLD ON. SO, YOU'VE BEEN TRAINING FOR TWENTY YEARS TO *KILL ME?*

...
...

BEWARE! MY CRONIES...

...WILL MAKE SOME *SERIOUS* MAYHEM WHEN THEY FIND YOU.

THEY'RE NO AMATEUR ASSASSINS. *BETTER WATCH OUT.*

YOU'RE **WAY** TOO *TRUSTING.*

I COULD SHOOT YOU IN THE BACK.

MY FINGER'S...

...ON THE TRIGGER, TOO.

WE WERE A *PART* OF THE *TOTAL DAMAGE.*

THIS TIME WE WERE CAUGHT UP, TOO.

NOTHING SEEMED OUT OF THE ORDINARY TO *EITHER* OF THEM.

WHAT WAS UP WITH THAT *COIN...?*

DON'T YOU *GET IT?!* EVERYONE'S SHAKEN.

WE CAN'T EVEN SLEEP AT NIGHT.

I SAY WE DO *SOMETHING* ABOUT IT. SOMEONE'S GOTTA TELL HIM TO GET *OUTTA HERE!*

UH...

VASH...

109

EEK!

.....

THOSE SCARS...

THAT'S THE *PRICE* YOU PAY FOR NOT *KILLING* YOUR OPPONENTS, ISN'T IT?

THAT IS *NOT* TRUE...

COME ON, *THEY WOULD NOT!*

THEY'D JUST RUN AWAY!

THIS STUFF'S NOT MEANT FOR THE TENDER EYES OF *LADIES.*

EVEN THOUGH YOU DON'T HAVE A *PRICE* ON YOUR HEAD ANYMORE!!

MAKE NO MISTAKE. THAT GUY WAS AIMING FOR *YOU.*

VASH-SAN...

JUST WHAT *IS* GOING ON?

112

IF I LIVE MY OWN LIFE NOW IN PEACE...

WOULD I BE ANY BETTER THAN A *LAZY PIG?*

I STILL HAVEN'T SETTLED THAT SCORE.

YOU LEAVIN'?

YEAH.

EH...

-:HUNNH:-

UP ON THE LEFT-HAND SIDE, SEMPAI!!!

HUH...

WHAT...!!

DON'T COME *ANY* CLOSER, YOU TWO!

STOP!

HUH?

...
...

HIS
FAVORITE
SUBORDI-
NATE...

DRIP

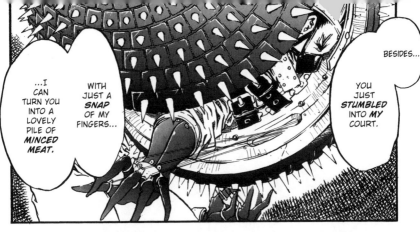

...I CAN TURN YOU INTO A LOVELY PILE OF *MINCED MEAT*.

WITH JUST A *SNAP* OF MY FINGERS...

YOU JUST *STUMBLED* INTO *MY* COURT.

BESIDES...

I HAVE ONLY TWO CHOICES: TO *DIE* OR LET *OTHERS* DIE?!

THAT SCENARIO'S *NO GOOD.*

HMM?

...DIDN'T SACRIFICE HER LIFE FOR THAT!

REM...

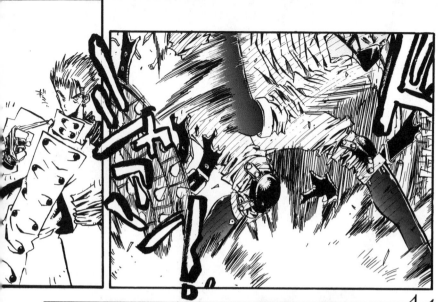

WHA--?!

EH?!

...

HEY!!

...

OH,
M--

127

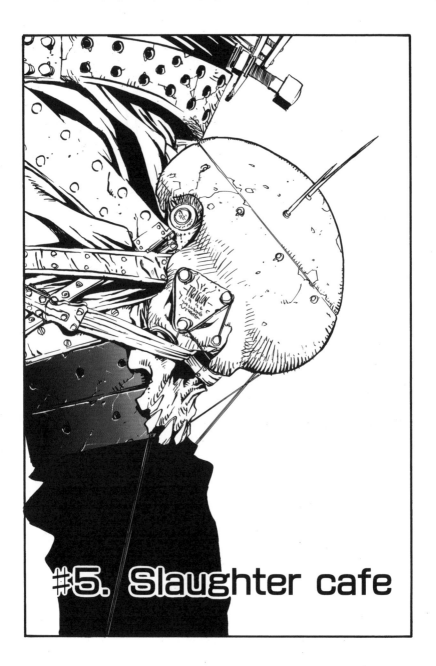

#5. Slaughter cafe

JENEORA
ROCK.

1000
KILOMETERS
NORTHWEST
OF MAY
CITY.

IT
SERVES
AS THE
RELAY
POINT TO
*AUGUSTA
CITY.*

...FROM TIME TO TIME, THE HOT WINDS...

...SUMMON VISITORS TO THIS SMALL COUNTRY TOWN.

NATURALLY...

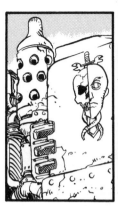

...I'M HUNTING YOU!!

FROM NOW ON...

BOOZE!

BRING US THE *BEST* IN THE *HOUSE!*

THA--

THAT'S THE *RODERICK SLAVE TRAFFICK-ERS!*

THOSE *PERVERTS* MUST ENJOY TREATING THEM LIKE *DIRT!!* MAKES ME WANNA *PUKE!!*

THOSE GIRLS MUST BE THEIR *CAPTIVES...*

SUCH SINNERS...

B... BAS- TARDS...

WE GOTTA HELP THEM *FORGET AGAIN!*

PLAYIN' *COOL,* HUH?

YOU SURE GOT *BALLS!*

SAY SOME-THING, YOU COCKY SONUVA--!

141

DON'T SCREW WITH ME!!

MADAM?

ANOTHER SPOON PL--

EVENTUALLY I WILL OBLITERATE EVERY *LAST TRACE* OF MANKIND.

WHY *MUST* YOU RUSH...

...THE *INEVITABLE*?

?!

WHA--?

TOO HASTY...

...YOU *MAGGOT!!*

IT WAS A GRUESOME, NIGHT-MARISH FIGHT.

THE *RODERICK GANG* ONLY KILLED ONE ANOTHER.

THE MAN CONTROLLED EVERYONE *SINGLE-HANDEDLY.*

THOSE WHO SAW EVERYTHING AT THE SCENE OF THE CRIME GAVE THIS TESTIMONY...

THAT WAS SO UNLIKE ME.

I DON'T USUALLY WASTE TIME ON VERMIN.

ISN'T THAT AMUSING, VASH THE STAMPEDE?

YOUR VERY EXISTENCE IS A NEVER-ENDING IRRITATION...

#5. Slaughter cafe/END

THE BUS CONTINUES NORTH-WEST.

IT'S 2000 KILOMETERS UNTIL *AUGUSTA.*

OH, I WANT TO KNOW...

#6. GATHERING OF THE DEVILS

...WHERE CAN I GET A NICE CUP OF *TEA?*

...THE **HELL** THAT AWAITED ME WOULD BEGIN.

IF I MOVED MY FOOT JUST A LITTLE...

I JUST HAD A **HUNCH**...

WHO WOULD FIGHT **THIS** GUY?!

YOU'RE THE **DEATH-WISH!**

PICKING A FIGHT WITH A GUY LIKE THAT?! THAT'S A **DEATH-WISH!**

... ...

WHAT CAN YOU DO?

WHAT A NIGHT-MARE...

WHEN I THINK ABOUT IT...

EH?!

...IT'S ALMOST TOO MUCH!

AAAH!

NOW WHAT ?!

WAAH!

THAT'S ONE **WELL-PREPARED** DEAD GUY.

⊰WHEW⊱ ....

SAVED...

I'M SAVED ...!!

....

...FROM WHERE MY *BIKE* BROKE DOWN.

I WALKED *ALL* THIS WAY...

IT MUST'VE BEEN *EXHAUSTING* TO WALK WITH THAT HUGE THING ON YOUR BACK...

I RECKON I *DO* HAVE MY *PRIDE* AS A *TRADES-MAN.*

YEAH.

TRADES-MAN?

I'M A *PRIEST !!*

O LORD, THIS WORLD'S *FULL* OF SUCH *PREJUDICE.*

AND WHAT KINDA CLERGYMAN DRESSES LIKE *THAT?!*

A PRIEST ISN'T A *TRADES-MAN.*

....

NO, NO, IT WASN'T US. THEY STOPPED THE BUS BECAUSE *SOMEONE* WAS MAKIN' *NOISE.*

HE'S THE ONE WHO SAW YOU WHEN YOU WERE JUST A *SPECK* ON THE *HORIZON!*

SO, THANKS.

YOU'RE THE ONES THAT FOUND ME, RIGHT? YOU SAVED MY LIFE.

159

....
...!

WAIT!

THAT
FLAG...

IS
THAT
A CARA-
VAN?

WHAT
THE
HELL IS
ALL THAT
RACKET
?!

IT'S THE
REST OF
*RODERICK'S
CREW!!*

DON'T YOU **SEE**?! THEY'RE GETTIN' **REVENGE** FOR THEIR BUDDIES YESTERDAY!

IT **CAN'T** BE **THEM**!

JUST WHAT THE **HELL** ARE YOU DOIN', **SHERIFF**?

YOU THAT **BASTARD'S PARTNER**? IT'S ODD YOU DIDN'T **ARREST** HIM.

HE'S A FREAKIN' **MESS**.

BOSS...

SHERIFF

THAT
ROOKIE...

WE'LL
TEACH
HIM
THERE'S
A PRICE
TO PAY...

THERE
ARE
SO
MANY
OF
YOU.

ARE YOU
MOVING
IN?

...
...

THAT
HAIR...

....
...!

THAT
WHITE
COAT
...!!

IT'S
YOU,
ISN'T
IT?!

AH, OF COURSE. YOU'RE IN LEAGUE WITH THOSE **WORMS** FROM YESTERDAY.

YOU SAID YOU WERE LOOKING FOR ME.

HAR
HAR
HAR

WELL THEN, YOU HAVE TWO POSSIBLE DESTINA- TIONS...

NO MATTER WHAT THEY SAY...

...I DON'T BELIEVE TH' BOSS WAS KILLED BY A **JERK** LIKE **YOU.**

APPAR- ENTLY A **POINT- LESS** QUESTION.

HMPH...

"HOME" OR THE "NEXT WORLD."

...DIE!

THEN...

NOT GOOD. I'LL STARVE AT THIS RATE.

MAKE ME A DEAL, DRIVER.

HMM...

ONE.

TWO.

THREE.

ER, FOUR.

OH, THAT'S RIGHT!

WHAT A LIFESAVER! THANKS!

REALLY?!

OKAY, YOU CAN RIDE FOR $$80.

WH-WH...

WHAT *IS* THIS?!

IT'S A *CONFESSIONAL.*

A PORTABLE VERSION OF THE BOX THEY HAVE IN CHURCH.

173

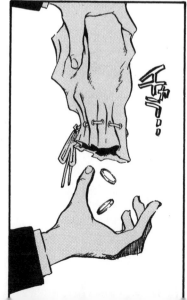

HEY, YOU GUYS SHOULDN'T DO THAT.

THAT MAN HAS NO MONEY.

THIS IS A PROBLEM.

OH, NO.

...IS MINE.

IT'S NOT MUCH, BUT WILL IT DO?

FINE...
COME GET
A BITE
TO EAT
WITH ME,
WOLFWOOD.

MY
TREAT,
OF
COURSE.

REALLY?!

SUCH
A GOOD
GUY!

AH!

AAA
AAH
HEH
AHA
HEH

AHA
HA
HA
HAHA

180

#6. GATHERING OF THE DEVILS/END

#7. EYE OF
INVISIBILITY

A SKULL ATTACHED TO HIS LEFT ARM?!

HUH?!

OUR TARGET...

...HAS YET TO ARRIVE.

"CHAPEL" SEEMS TO BE MISSING...

WELL, NO MATTER.

WELL, IF YOU SEE HIM, LET ME KNOW.

YOU DON'T KNOW HIM?

AND A RAISED, NEEDLE-LIKE TORTURE DEVICE ON HIS RIGHT SHOULDER.

....

YEP, YEP!

THAT'S RIGHT.

WEREN'T YOU *THERE* THAT *TIME*?

WHAT DO YOU MEAN *"WHAT AM I SAYING"*?

WHAT ARE YOU SAYING?

WHO'S THAT? A FRIEND OF YOURS?

HEY, HEY...

188

NO, WAIT...

DID HE **REALLY** DISGUISE HIMSELF THAT EASILY?!

OR MAYBE...

HEY, HEY! ARE YOU TWO SERIOUS?!!

...

...

? ?

...HE MADE HIMSELF INVISIBLE TO OTHERS!!

THOUGH I WAS LOOKING RIGHT AT HIM...

WELL?

IF HE... IF HE CAN MOVE IN AND OUT OF A CROWD LIKE THAT, PEOPLE CAN BE KILLED **EASILY**...

LIKE A SHADOW, HE CAME.

EH!!

IF I SEE THAT GUY, WHAT SHOULD I DO? YOU GOT A MESSAGE FOR HIM?

NO! NO! NEVER-MIND!!

AND LIKE A SHADOW, HE KILLED AND SLIPPED AWAY.

191

EH? YOU'RE *LEAVING?*

DUTY CALLS.

THANKS, IT WAS FUN.

I'LL BE HEADIN' ALONG NOW.

IF A GOOD WIND BLOWS, I'LL MEET YOU AGAIN.

MAY THE LORD'S *DIVINE PROTECTION* BE WITH YOU!

WHERE...

...IS HE?

YOU'RE THE ONE WHO *UPPED* THE *ANTE.*

I WON'T FOLD WHILE THE CARDS ARE STILL FACE-DOWN.

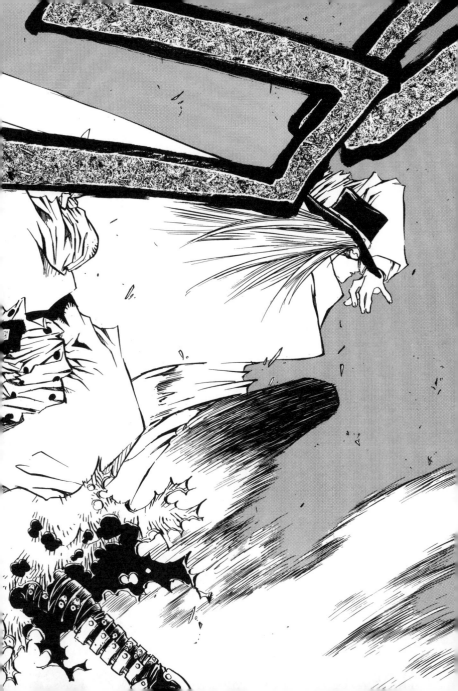

WELL, THIS AIN'T ANY FUN.

WITH THE CHURCH UP SO HIGH, IT'S *NO WONDER* THE CONGREGATION'S SHRINKIN'.

.....

.....

THERE'S NO ONE 'ROUND...

WHAT WAS *THAT?*

GUN-SHOTS?!

211

YOU'RE AN UNPREDICTABLE MAN.

I'M UNPREDICTABLE?!

I'M NOT THE ONE TELEPORTING *ALL OVER* THE PLACE!

I LIKE IT.

DAMMIT, THOSE ARE FIGHTING WORDS.

....
....

I WONDER HOW LONG YOU CAN KEEP IT UP.

....
....

IF YOU GET THE CHANCE...

...GO AHEAD AND *SHOOT ME.*

THAT'S *TWICE* SHE'S FOOLED MY EYES ALREADY.

BUT NOW I KNOW SHE'S GOT A *CARD OR TWO* UP HER SLEEVE.

KNOWING THAT MAKES *ALL* THE DIFFERENCE IN THE WORLD.

YOU'RE PRETTY *CONFIDENT.*

BUT I *DON'T* THINK IT WILL WORK.

I *MUST* TAKE HER DOWN.

BY ANY MEANS NECESSARY.

YOU *CAN'T* BEAT ME, EVEN WITH SPEED ON YOUR SIDE!

HAVEN'T I TOLD YOU?

LOOK! LOOK! LOOK!

SHE'S GOING TO MOVE. DON'T MISS IT!

216

YOU'RE *VERY* SLOPPY. YOU MADE ME MISS *TWICE*...

HAA...

HAA...

HAA...

....

..?!

SLOPPY? WHO MISSED?

HOW DOES SHE *DO* THAT?

I'M PAYING ATTENTION, BUT WHEN SHE MOVES, IT'S LIKE SHE'S NOT EVEN *THERE*!!

#7:EYE OF INVISIBILITY/END

#8. FIFTH MOON

HYPNOSIS--

...
...

I HURT MY FINGER EARLIER.

HOW?!

HOW'D YOU...

ESCAPE IT?!

SH--!!

YOU HAD ME UNDER YOUR *SPELL.*

YOU INDUCED *SENSORY PARALYSIS,* AM I RIGHT?

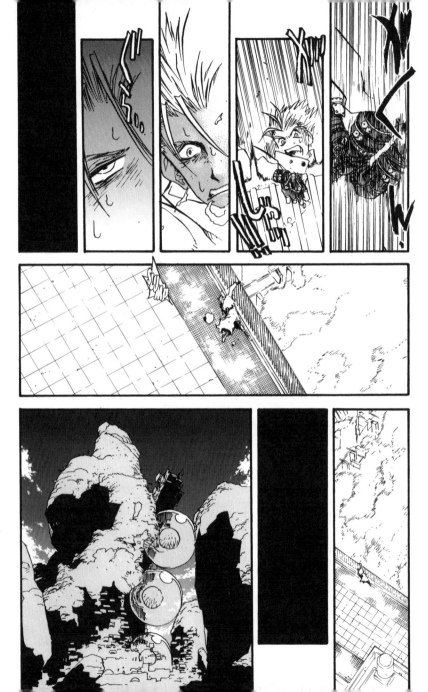

BECAUSE I MERELY WANT HIM *CONFINED.*

AND *CLOSELY GUARDED.*

PLEASE, TELL ME.

WHY YOU DO NOT *SUMMON* US?

DOMINIQUE IS DONE FOR...

OH, WELL. HER TIME RAN OUT.

...

THE *"DOCTOR"* CAN EXPLAIN IN DETAIL.

IT SEEMS HE'S ARRIVED...

....
....

YOUR **WORK** IS APPRECIATED, LEGATO.

IT SEEMS THAT WE DON'T HAVE MUCH TIME...

WE MUST REVIVE THE BODY OF **KNIVES** TODAY.

236

IT'S A GAMBLE, BUT BY SYNCHING HIM WITH THE *"PLANT,"* HE **COULD** BE RESURRECTED.

WE CAN NO LONGER **USE** THE **ORIGINAL** BODY.

YOU MUST BE READY TO HANDLE **ANY** SITUATION...

WE'RE ENTERING **UNKNOWN TERRITORY** HERE.

YOU ALL WERE SUMMONED FOR A PURPOSE. TOGETHER, NOTHING CAN STOP YOU.

ESPECIALLY...

HE'S COMING... ISN'T HE...

I UNDER-STAND WHY **KNIVES** CHOSE THIS PLACE...

BY **NO MEANS** MAY YOU **FAIL!!**

...VASH THE STAMPEDE.

...WHY IS HE PULLING HIM HERE?

IF THEY'RE FAMILY...

ONCE IT'S GONE FULL CIRCLE...

ONCE AGAIN, I'M STAINING MY **OWN HANDS** WITH BLOOD.

SHIT!

WHAT THE **HELL** WAS WITH ALL TH' TRAINING?!

...WHERE WILL IT END?

GOD...

THAT'S JUST IT, ISN'T IT?

AFTER ALL THIS TIME, WHAT'S IT **WORTH?**

...
...

IF I RUN...

IN THE DESERT NIGHT, IT'S EASY TO FEAR THE **"DISCIPLES"** ON THIS MOUNTAIN...

AND IN THE END, CAN I **ESCAPE?**

I'LL BE DEVOURED...

I KNOW...

IT'S...
YOU...

YOU'VE
COME...

WHA!
WHA-
WHA-
WHA-
WHA-
WHA--

VA!
VA-
VA-
VA-
VA-
VA--

243

SEMPA!!

THERE'S MAJOR CHAOS OUT-SIDE!!

YOU CAN'T! NOT IN YOUR CONDITION!! DON'T GET UP, YOU'RE EXHAUSTED!

VASH-SAN!!

GET YOURSELVES AWAY FROM HERE!!

HURRY AND ESCAPE!!

DIDN'T I TELL YOU NOT TO MOVE?! AREN'T YOU LISTENING TO ME?!

GET THE HELL OUT OF HERE!!

YOU'RE THE ONE WHO'S GONE DEAF!!

I LET
HIM
GO...

WHY?

MAYBE I
WAS TOO
TIRED.

THIS PLACE
IS GONNA
BLOW *SKY-
HIGH.*

GET
YOURSELVES
TO A SAFE
PLACE.

THAT
MAN...

...CALLED
ME BY
**MY
NAME**
FOR THE
VERY
FIRST
TIME.

WHO'S THAT, MAN...?

I'VE SEEN HIM BEFORE.

HEY, KNIVES!

...

...!!

...ON THESE HUMANS.

USE IT...

SOMETHING'S... RISING TO THE SURFACE!!

WAIT!!

WAIT. WAIT. WAIT.

SOMETHING... UNBELIEVABLE... SOMETHING SICK...

REM...
...

REM...
...

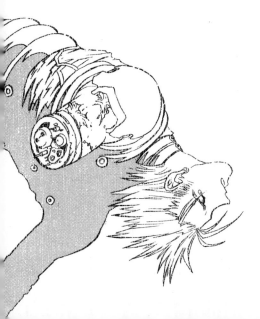

WE

MAYBE   *I*

*SHOULD
HAVE
NEVER
BEEN*

BORN.

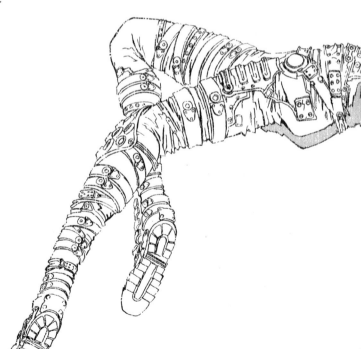

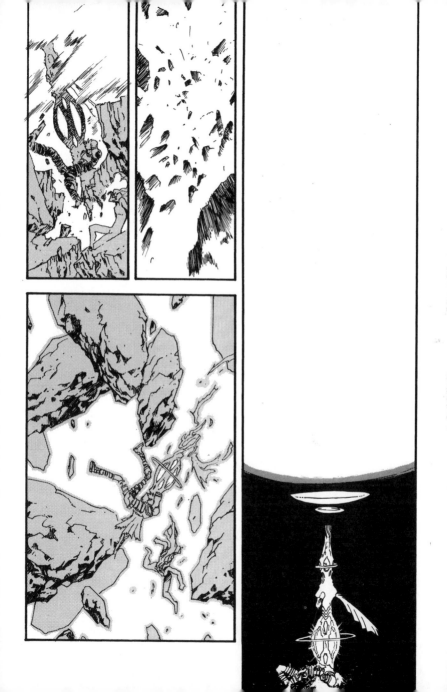

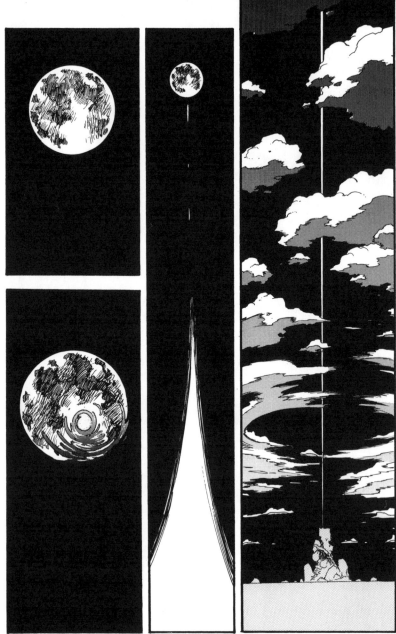

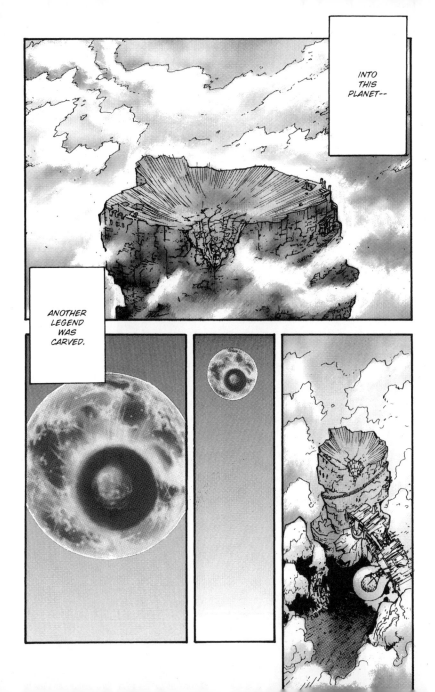

INTO
THIS
PLANET--

ANOTHER
LEGEND
WAS
CARVED.

THE PEOPLE DREW EVER CLOSER.

THEY WERE COMPELLED TO.

THE "MARK" IMPOSED AN INCREDIBLE POWER.

THOSE WORDS ROLLED LIKE A SMALL WAVE.

BUT THEY SOON COVERED THE PLANET.

SOMEONE MURMURED...

..."THE DEVIL IS REAL."

FROM
THAT BODY
THE GRIM
REAPER GAVE
BIRTH TO
CHAOS--

WOULD
HE DARE
MOW US ALL
DOWN WITH
*DEATH'S
SCYTHE?*

NO ONE KNOWS THE WHERE-ABOUTS OF THAT MAN.

THE LAST TWO YEARS OF **VASH THE STAMPEDE'S** FOOTSTEPS WERE **ERASED** FROM OUR HISTORY...

#8. FIFTH MOON/END

TURN TO THE MAXIMUM
TRIGUN YASUHIRO NIGHTOW

TRIGUN
BONUS
TRACKS!!
YASUHIRO NIGHTOW

TRIGUN

特別編

DAY IN DAY OUT

AS A BOY, THIS WALKING DISASTER ROAMED FREE. WHAT DID HE THINK ABOUT? WHAT DID HE DO?

THERE ONCE WAS A MAN...

THIS TIME, LET'S TAKE A LOOK AT THE VASH YOU NEVER KNEW!!

THE FIRST MAN EVER TO BE DECLARED A NATURAL DISASTER, VASH THE STAMPEDE.

EARLIER THAN
THE ROOSTER'S
CROW, CHILDREN
ON SUNDAY, AND
THE MORNING
PAPER.

VASH THE
STAMPEDE
GETS UP
EARLY
IN THE
MORNING--

MORNING MEDITATION THEME: "LIFE AND LOVE."

THREE SECONDS.

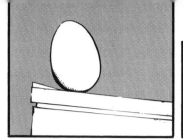

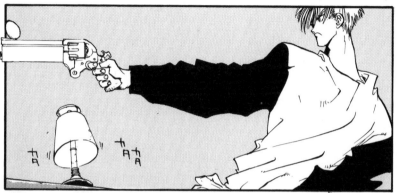

TECHNIQUE
TRAINING:
THREE
HOURS.

-->HUP!<--

-->HUP!<--

-->HUP!<--

-->HOOMPH!<--

-->HOOMPH!<--

-->HOOMPH!<--

-->HOOMPH!<--

--SMITH?!

--?

RIGHT!!

OH YES, AT THAT TIME HE WAS USING AN ALIAS!!

MR. JOHN P. SMITH (ALIAS)

GOOD MORNING, MISTER SMITH.

YOU SURE GET UP EARLY, DON'T YOU?

IF HE USES HIS REAL NAME, PEOPLE NEVER TRUST HIM.

HA! HAHAHAHA! NO, I DON'T! GIMME A BREAK! HOLD ON NOW...

GEEZ! YOU LOOK LIKE HIM! THAT GUY! YEAH! JUST LIKE HIM!

AT FIRST, HE AND TROUBLE ARE A WEIRD COMBINATION.

WHAT WITH THAT CRAZY HAIR AND ALL...

HE THINKS ABOUT IT OVER BREAKFAST...

CHOMP

CHOMP

HE CAN'T SIMPLY LIVE AS AN AVERAGE, HONEST PERSON.

SO, YOU'VE COME...!!

....

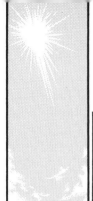

ROCK! PAPER! SCISSORS!

UNTIL NOON...

HE TAKES HIS CHANCES AT CHESS WITH THE NEIGHBORHOOD OLD MAN.

AH! OW-OW-OW-OW!

YAR!

AFTERNOON-- HE PLAYS COPS AND ROBBERS WITH THE KIDS COMING HOME FROM SCHOOL.

FROM HIS FIRST DAY IN TOWN, HE LET THEM GET HIM GOOD.

12:30...

HE LOSES $55.

...

WATCH OUT!

SO SORRY...

YOU OKAY?!

ドドドドドドド

STAY OUT OF *TROUBLE*, STAY *ALIVE.*

DON'T BE A *FOOL.*

WHAT THE HELL, *BRO?*

DON'TCHA GOT ANY *GUTS?*

GAH! ADULTS SAY SUCH *STUPID* THINGS!!

...
...

WHILE THE PEOPLE BEND THEIR EARS TO LISTEN TO THE SATELLITE BROADCAST OF "ALL DAYS"...

AND THEN, THAT NIGHT...

IF I EVER MEET THAT KID, *I'LL* TAKE 'IM OUT WITH *JUST ONE SHOT!*

HA!

I HEAR IT WAS THAT *NEBRASKA PAIR* AT WORK!

GIMME A BREAK! *"HUMANOID TYPHOON"!*

JUST BECAUSE ONE *SCRAWNY* TOWN WAS *WIPED OUT!!*

AND ISN'T HE A MAN WITHOUT *BLOOD* OR *TEARS?!*

MY CHILDREN AND I WILL *PERISH!*

YOU HAVEN'T GOT THE *SKILL!* DON'T GET THIS *WHOLE* TOWN CRUSHED!

DON'T BE AN IDIOT!

OW-OW-OW-OW!

SHUT UP!

OLD HAG...

YOU MOUTHY--

DI--

KYAAA! SODOM DARLING, ARE YOU OKAY?!

VASH THE STAMPEDE.

AAH! HEY! HEY!

HE MADE IT THROUGH ANOTHER DAY WITH NO CASUALTIES. NICELY DONE!

WELL, SEE YOU NEXT TIME!!

--IE!! OOF!

...
...

■DAY IN DAY OUT /END

WE FELL FROM THE SKY LIKE DROPLETS OF RAIN.

LANDING ON THIS DESERT PLANET, BURNED BY THE DAYTIME SUN. WHO KNOWS WHEN WE'LL DRY UP...

TRIGUN PILOT

EVEN IF WE'RE SHELTERED BENEATH A GIANT UMBRELLA, WE DON'T KNOW WHAT TOMORROW MAY HOLD.

SOMEDAY, EVERYONE COULD BE BLOWN BY THE DESERT WIND AND SUCKED INTO THE SAND.

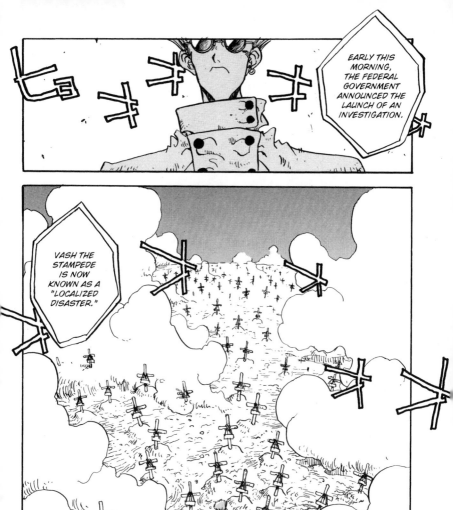

EARLY THIS MORNING, THE FEDERAL GOVERNMENT ANNOUNCED THE LAUNCH OF AN INVESTIGATION.

VASH THE STAMPEDE IS NOW KNOWN AS A "LOCALIZED DISASTER."

THERE ARE *THREE THINGS* IN THIS WORLD THAT I *CAN'T* STAND.

AND *BASTARDS* WHO DON'T KNOW THE VALUE OF *PEACE 'N' QUIET!*

SCORPION-LIKE PATTERNS...

PUTTING ICE IN BOOZE...

EVERYONE ELSE SAYS A CARD-LOVING GIRL IS AMONG THE HOSTAGES, *COUNT BOSTALK.*

I'VE PUT TOGETHER ALL THE WITNESSES' STATE-MENTS.

FIVE PEOPLE DIDN'T GET OUT IN TIME.

A *ROBBERY* IN MY JURIS-DICTION?!

NOT ON *MY* WATCH!!!

THEY'LL **USE** MY DAUGHTER AND THEN **DUMP HER** IN THE DESERT.

IF WORD LEAKS OUT, EVERY **SCUMBAG** WILL COME LOOKING FOR **EASY MONEY.**

THEY **WON'T** GET AWAY WITH THIS!

THEY DEMAND A GETAWAY WAGON AND $$400,000 **RANSOM.**

YOU'D BETTER THINK ABOUT HOW TO GET MY DAUGHTER OUT SAFELY.

WATCH YOUR **MOUTH,** SHERIFF.

YOU SPEAK LIKE YOU KNOW A THING OR TWO, **"GRIMREAPER BOSTALK."**

AH!!

YOU DON'T GIVE ME ORDERS.

I DON'T CARE HOW MANY OTHERS HAVE TO DIE.

DON'T LOSE TRACK OF WHAT'S IMPORTANT!

HE'S JUST PLAIN STUPID, BOSS!!

NOTHING PLAIN ABOUT THE RUCKUS HE'S MAKING.

ROBBERS! SOME-BODY SAVE ME!!!

WAAAAAAH!!

306

WHY ELSE WOULD THEY *HOLD UP* THIS DIVE?

THEY'RE *AFTER* MY FAMILY'S MONEY.

THESE GUYS...

SHE'S YOUR WARN- ING!!!

THIS *"LADY"*?

WHOA, HOW SAD!!

...THAT I LET SUCH A THING HAPPEN TO YOU.

MY *SINCEREST* APOLOGIES, MISS...

WELL, GO ON WITH YOUR PLAN.

BETTER NOT ASK FOR ANYTHING *STUPID.* IF IT'S A LITTLE MONEY YOU WANT, I CAN GET PAPA TO HAND IT OVER.

SAY...

WANNA GET MARRIED?

YES! JUST NOT TO A *MORON!!!*

I SEE...

YOUR FAMILY'S LOADED...

308

310

311

I'M SORRY! I'M SORRY!

THAT WAS YOU?!

YOU SCARED ME, YOU *BASTARD!*

GUM?

...?

...
...

COULDN'T BE...

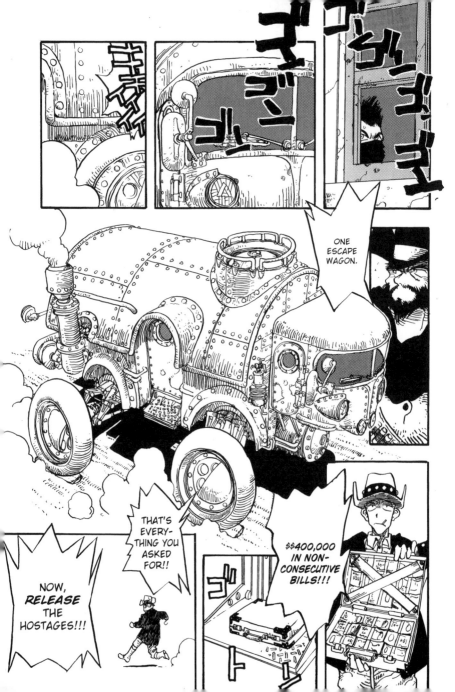

ONE ESCAPE WAGON.

THAT'S EVERY-THING YOU ASKED FOR!!

$$400,000 IN NON-CONSECUTIVE BILLS!!!

NOW, *RELEASE* THE HOSTAGES!!!

BE CAREFUL.

I'M GOING.

DON'T TRY ANYTHING!

NOT *YET!!* WE'VE GOTTA INSPECT THE VEHICLE AND THE MONEY!!!

TR...

...?!

316

!!

YOU OKAY?

YES...

Y....

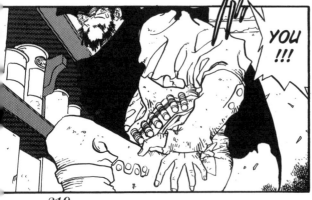

YOU !!!

KYA AA AA A!

ALL I REMEMBER IS THEM WORKING, COVERED IN DIRT...

BUT AFTER TEN YEARS, THEY MADE THIS SANDY SOIL FERTILE. IT WAS A HUGE ACCOMPLISHMENT.

Y'KNOW THAT BIG GRAVEYARD NORTHEAST OF HERE?

THAT'S WHERE OUR FATHERS ARE BURIED.

IT'S SO BARREN THAT EVEN CORPSE WEEDS WON'T GROW.

GET IT NOW? PAPA NEVER INTENDED TO PAY YOU!!!

ALL YOUR PARTNERS ARE DEAD. IF YOU KEEP THIS UP...

-WHEW-

DON'T LOOK AWAY.

...
...

FORGIVE ME.

YOU HAVE WHAT YOU WANT. LET THE GIRL GO.

TRUE.

...THOSE ON WHOM YOUR LIFE WAS BUILT?

I DON'T THINK YOU'RE STUPID ENOUGH TO IGNORE...

THIS GUY...

HE'S *ACTUALLY* CRYING.

I REALLY HATE SEEING PEOPLE DIE.

SO SENSE-LESS...

IF I SHUT YOU TWO UP, THIS *WHOLE* TOWN WILL BE *MINE.*

I NEVER IMAGINED I'D HAVE THE CHANCE.

I'M TRULY SURPRISED

328

...PEACE!

A MAN WHOSE NAME MEANS "RECK-LESS."

VASH THE STAMPEDE

LOVE AND...

SHORTLY AFTER, HE WAS DECLARED...

...MANKIND'S FIRST "LOCALIZED DISASTER."

■TRI GUN／END

WELCOME TO THE FUTURE #2

ORIGINAL TITLE: THE SPIRAL OF LIFE #2

I AM YASUHIRO NIGHTOW (33). I WAS DESCRIBING THE PROCESS OF DEVELOPING MY STORY WHEN THE PUBLISHER CAME ALONG, SHOUTED AND PUNCHED ME...

YOU HAVE NO DREAMS, NO WILL, NO *INNER* FIRE!!

YOU DON'T EVEN EXERCISE. YOU ARE WASTING YOUR LIFE AWAY!

YOU EAT, SLEEP, GAME, SLEEP, AND ONLY WRITE A LITTLE BIT IN BETWEEN.

NO MATTER HOW MANY YEARS PASS, IF MY LIFE CONTINUES TO BE A WASTE, WHAT DOES THAT MAKES YOURS?

BUT...

THAT MIGHT BE SO...

WOULD YOU LIKE...

...SOME TEA PERHAPS?

BON VOYAGE, ST. ELMO'S FIRE--

WAIT OLD MAN...

IN MY OLD AGE, THIS IS ALL I HAVE BECOME.

HE JUST MADE A GOOD POINT, NYA~

YOU... YOUR YOUTH...

I LOST...

SAY OLD MAN...

OLD MAN, AREN'T YOU IN CHARGE OF MY FUTURE?

STOP CALLING ME OLD MAN!

....
....

I DON'T UNDERSTAND...

IF ONLY I COULD DEFY TIME WITH A COMPRESSION FREEZER, LIKE KATSUMIRA MIKA...

HA HA! I CAN'T TELL YOU THAT.

WHAT DOES MY FUTURE HOLD?

I'LL ASK YOU DIRECTLY.

YEAH.

ARE YOU GOING HOME NOW?

I SEE.

I'M THE SAME WAY.

DO YOU LIKE DRAWING MANGA?

...

I LIKE IT.

SOMETIMES... I HATE IT.

⚠ STOP
This is the back of the book!

This manga collection is translated into English but oriented in right-to-left reading format at the creator's request, maintaining the artwork's visual orientation as originally published in Japan. If you've never read manga in this way before, take a look at the diagram below to give yourself an idea of how to go about it. Basically, you'll be starting in the upper right corner and will read each balloon and panel moving right to left. It may take some getting used to, but you should get the hang of it very quickly. Have fun!

D0908513